T0066793

One Life

One Life

In Conversation with You

Saim A. Khan

PARTRIDGE

To order additional copies of this book, contact
Partridge India
000 800 10062 62
orders.india@partridgepublishing.com

www.partridgepublishing.com/india

Contents

Introduction

Who am I? What's my purpose, past life, rebirth, life after death, parallel worlds, astral travels, and future?

These are all in reference to various faiths and beliefs, and for all our respect to these relative realities, we usually undermine our present existence—this life, *one life*.

How easy it is to just forget about ourselves and be so involved and engrossed in everything but our own selves, and when we do realize this ignorance, we waste yet another number of years just to cover up the lost time and more years in search for our purpose, later wanting to have another life just to fulfil the one we lost or, better said, the one that faded into nothing.

Life is empty if happiness is not a constant in all the years it's made up of.

Past life or rebirth is a phase which you will take care of yourself but only at that moment, in that life, if it happens or had happened.

What you can do for yourself right now is what matters.

Bring chances and choices in your life and expand its possibilities, and to make it happen, all it requires is a change in perception. Change your perception, and you will change your entire life.

Now, today is what we have to live for, and don't just live it but live it the right way, the way that satisfies *you*, makes *you* happy, gives meaning to *your* existence, and gives it the name life, *your* life, *one life*.

Strength

While growing up, you take up activities, make friends, indulge in hobbies, and seek things that entertain you just to identify yourself; hence, this way you get to know the rights and wrongs for your life.

You don't build preconceived ideas about things you face. Everyone and everything is relative, entirely depending on your perception on that specific given time.

You have to hold on to yourself and not on your relative facts or fictions. Dreams come and go; times come and go, good or bad—all of it. The only constant one in all of it is you, yourself. That's all. And no experience can make you or break you; all it does is give you more awareness.

At the same time, you are naive to what was not offered to you, so you can't be biased.

Every step in tomorrow is a step in the dark. The choice is yours whether you want be lost in it or be found.

Don't regret what you lost because it makes you underestimate the gains of the future, which you're not even aware of.

Irrespective of phases, times do change, but only if you remain the same; it makes you superior to time.

It's difficult but not impossible.

Most of the time, you subconsciously tell yourself that you are not strong enough to face the challenges in life, but when you are strong enough to admit that you are not strong enough, then you decide for yourself how contradictions can merge. In your prayers, you always ask for strength, and only when you know what you want, that's when you get it. You know what you want; you want strength. When you have strength, you have everything. But the point is, you already have strength; you just need to recognize it and embrace it.

Strength is not how you hold on to things; it's how you get to those things. Securing something needs awareness, whereas achieving that something requires strength. Strength is neither innate nor sudden; it's built gradually and slowly with various ups and downs in life.

Strength is not something you are born with; strength is something you live with and die with.

Selflessness Survives on Selfishness

In life, you have many people who love you truly and care for you, like your family, few friends, and your spouse.

But when you are on your deathbed, no one's true love, extreme care, or affections can save your life. All you'll have at that moment will be your past, the memories of the life you lived. They'll make you either a happy person dying or a sad person dying.

So always make sure that whatever you do in life, it should make you happy, and once you are happy inside, only then can you make others happy too.

Family, friends, and spouse are no good if you can't keep them happy. It's like being surrounded by wrapped gifts and not even opening them to see what's inside. There is presence of love, but you just can't feel it.

Happiness is what brings out the best in people, be it a few close ones or even distant acquaintances. But in order to make others happy, first find ways to keep yourself happy.

It's said that being selfish is not good. But selfishness is misunderstood.

Selflessness survives on selfishness.

If you are happy, only then can you make others happy.

If you have money, only then can you help the needy.

If you are at peace within yourself, only then can you bring peace to your surroundings.

If anything you do for anybody makes you in any way feel good or gives you the slightest of satisfaction, it means your actions brought you happiness, and that means self-interest, hence selfishness. But on the other side, those same selfish actions brought somebody else happiness as well, and that's selflessness. There are no other ways to understand this simple truth.

As long as you are not harming anyone while fulfilling your own self-interest, you are not doing anything wrong.

It's very important to fill yourself with something which you plan to give to others, be it love, care, wealth, health, or your positivity.

Once you are filled inside and overflowing of it, all the ill feelings towards any other dissolves, and only the best of you is left for everyone to receive, see, and feel.

The Unexplainable Emotions

Feeling something strongly means a lot, if decoded correctly.

For instance, there are some things you don't question, some things you don't answer, and some things you don't reason because somewhere, deep down, you believe that all your true desires are actually possible.

'Start by doing what's necessary, then do what's possible and suddenly you are doing the impossible' (St Francis of Assisi).

You feel so much inside and have so many overwhelming ambitions yet no words to justify them; it's just like keeping a tiger in the city—too much energy and visions of higher grounds but still no means to realize it.

It's not easily possible, yet as the famous quote goes, 'Whatever the mind can conceive and believe, it can achieve' (Napoleon Hill).

You can and you will do whatever you want to as long as you know what you want to do. It's like you make up your mind, and all forces of nature are with you until you achieve it.

If it was easy, you wouldn't have cherished it.

If you cross the lake of fire from the side, you have achieved nothing. But if you walk through it on a wooden bridge, it's an achievement. Feel the heat.

It's the same thing but done differently with unbelievable results.

What you're going to do is a mystery. What you did is history, so don't get tangled in between. Just do what makes you happy. See what inspires you and feel what enlightens you.

You have enough years to realize your dreams irrespective of your age; there is always time for one more round.

Don't waste your time thinking of what you could have, would have, or should have done. Think about what you can, should, and will do now, and without any hesitation, go for your desired venture.

You often step back with the thought 'What if I am wrong?'

The point is, nothing happens if you are wrong; the question is, what if you were right?

If you want the regular, day-to-day, inconsequential life, then think about what-ifs and buts, and if you want something larger than that, remove those self-generated obstacles.

Most of your life, you keep judging yourself that you will either be successful or might just land up in the mediocre slot. You don't give yourself an opportunity to just be yourself and to let your life take shape as it has to while doing what makes you happy. There is a constant self-created pressure surrounding you that stops you from experiencing the simple and finer things of life, like just being happy with yourself and letting your mind free.

One failure is one step closer to the breakdown of dreams, but with biased opinions about yourself, you are failing even before you are starting.

Being afraid that you will fail and end up in the middle of nowhere, you give up, assuming security based on not even attempting something which could have turned positive.

Normally, the biggest fear in people is of facing fear itself or dreading the fact that they could end up having fears of so and so, inviting fear for no reason. This is fear of losing to uncertainty. But you should only be afraid when you have something to lose; one should not be afraid of losing something which one doesn't desire to start with. Dreaming and aspiring to reach some place other than your current one means that you don't desire your current situation; hence, don't be afraid of losing it for something you're going to gain.

Living in fear, which can be of anything, is the most destructive poison you can ever offer your life.

Only if you recognize the brighter side of that fear can it be of any use. There is an unstoppable force hidden in those fears. All you need to do is open your eyes and gather your strength, and your fear will change its form.

Know your path and walk on it alone. Many lives would run parallel, but never make those paths cross one another. You might lose the flavour of your individuality.

This is what is to be believed and followed.

Unfold Your Fears

One can never value something they possess until there is a fear of losing it.

Most of your life, you live with fear, but you just don't let courage surface itself, ignoring the fact that fear is the stepping stone for courage.

When you think it's over, the next step is success. It's just not a motivating statement but a fact as courage is what makes dreams into reality. Success is relative, entirely depending on the dreams you see and fulfil.

But what is courage?

It's the force of emotions which carries you to your desired destinations, running over obstacles and not stopping for anything negative. Its existence is noticed in life when you see the presence of fear—the fear of losing something, the fear of unseen or unknown forces, the fear of just about anything. And only when you accept the fear you have in you can courage start making a place for itself in your life.

Fear can't exist if courage is in you, and courage cannot enter your life if you don't acknowledge the fears, big or small, as *fear is the heartbeat of courage.*

Emotions Explained

The world's most powerful force, the most constructive and most destructive medium, is *human emotions.*

Human emotions are the fuel for your soul and your existence. It cannot be seen, nor can it be heard, but it can only be felt. Your actions, your behaviour, your talk, your thinking—everything is made up of emotions. It's your emotions that make you or break you. When you feel your heart is broken, when you feel lightness in your stomach, when you feel the pressure in your mind, they are your emotions making themselves felt.

Only true and honest love can achieve true and honest love in return. Hate can only be resolved by emotions of empathy and compassion.

Neither great power nor any amount of money can mould or buy the true and deep emotions of a human. No matter which walk of life you come from, how rich or how poor you are, how weak or how powerful you are, you can only attract emotions via emotions. The greatest power in this world is emotions; they are dynamic. Sometimes for a moment they can be stirred by external pressures or outer shows, but deep down, they can only be moved by their own kind—plain, simple, and honest emotions.

The love for power over another, over anything possibly created by humans, is also driven by emotions; no muscle or army can change that. And if only that basic emotion were diverted in the correct direction, it would take no time for this world to actually achieve true peace and happiness.

Everyone has a good side and a bad side in them, and if someone behaves badly with you, don't blame him or her for being ill-mannered. Maybe, just maybe, you failed to take out the good in them and attracted the bad side. Try changing your emotions. Make them pure and honest, and you will see the good in others; you will even see others being good to you.

The world in all its diversities is running because of human emotions. Be true to yourself by being true to your basic instincts, which is actually a way for your inner emotions to make you feel their presence, and you will get the best of everyone.

Hate attracts hate, love attracts love, and human attracts human. Choose wisely what you want to attract in your life.

Steps in Life

There are three *steps in life*: reality, illusion, and delusion.

Reality is who you are, what you have, where you are, what you do, and everything that exists in your moving life. It's relative yet constant for you.

Illusions are mostly misinterpreted as something that don't exist, which is true but in a healthy way. Illusions are your dreams, your aspirations, your ambitions, and your world, where you can even paint the impossible. And the silver lining in illusions is that they are possible as they are connected to your reality. Anything that you dream, anything that you aspire, you can achieve with dedication and hard work, and you can bring your illusions into your fast-moving reality.

But delusions are dangerous. They are fictions surviving on illusions, not at all connected to your reality. Once you enter the world of delusions, there is no turning back, and there is no moving forward. It's like a trap where the foundation is your imagination, its reach is as well an imagination, and you are like a cloud of no consequence stuck in between with no substance.

If you do move past delusions, you won't reach reality again because it's not a circle. You will reach delusional reality, which under any circumstances is more or less equal to extinction of your individuality.

Living in the moment and dreaming for the future is the most credible approach to your life. But it has to be restricted and organized because there is only one step between illusions and delusions. It's very subtle, and most people cross it and lose their existing reality forever.

Different Faces of Life

At times, you have déjà vu, or you have a feeling that someone you just met is one you have known before or that a place you have just seen is one you have already been to before. In your subconscious mind, you have some vision, and you actually come across the same vision sometime later.

All this has happened with me before (and with you too), and I feel that though I was born a number of years ago, my soul must be older.

Your soul is the essence of your existence. It's the source in you which makes you choose the right and the wrong in your life. It's often referred to as gut, but it's actually your novice or wise soul guiding you. The soul is the energy and the real you connected with the divine with no in-between. You don't need to connect with the energies that surround you. You need to connect with the soul within you, and you are connected to all the energies around you.

Give your soul a chance.

'I was better in my past.' You should never compare your present self to your past self. Yesterday is history. Learn something, but never try to compare yourself. Live accordingly.

People say you are a loser, that you haven't achieved anything, but this is only because the path you have chosen is offbeat and different from the ones passing their opinions.

Your path is not what the world follows. So you have to face these side effects created by crowds of hundreds, such as feeling alone, weekends at home, going to bed early. You try to reach out to people or your apparent friends, but everyone is busy doing something, and unfortunately, you are not a part of it.

Most of the time, it feels like either you are crazy or the people around you are crazy, but as a matter of fact, no one is crazy.

It's such a feeling because you are like fire in the middle of the ocean, worlds apart but still one of the faces of nature.

Know Your Questions

This is one rule I always followed in life: To get the correct answer, you should know the correct question.

Ask yourself if you know your point right. Then to every answer, there should be a question with another answer.

Always think, rethink, and be sure of yourself before a word spoken because once you are aware of what you're talking, knowing all its possibilities, you can talk about it with millions of people and can get your point across everyone without any positive or negative debate.

Many times it happens that you are in a discussion and, as you are agreeing or disagreeing with the ongoing topic, are asked about your opinion and why.

You end up short of words for the simple reason that you have not been listening, and even if you have been listening, then you have not been understanding. You don't even raise the point that you are unable to understand because you don't want to sound unaware. But because of this action, you come across as gullible and very hazy in your mind.

There is no harm in asking repeatedly as it is through debates and conversations that the mind opens and builds up space for brilliance to settle itself. Even at the risk of sounding stupid, you can ask again.

Asking something does not challenge your intelligence, but unable to answer the questions raised in your conversation will definitely generate doubts about your intelligence.

Finding the Purpose of Life

By thinking and believing that you don't have a dream or purpose or the passion to pursue one is actually the best platform to achieve one as when you have nothing to lose, all is to gain. The suffocation between this doubt and confusion gives you the courage to generate an ounce of belief in yourself, and that will find you places and ways you've never even imagined nor ever heard of. All you have to do is what you have to do, and once trying to do that, passing various phases and emotions, you find one constant in all. That becomes your 'will' to ascend.

You have to dream your dream to actually fulfil it. Make your mind see it, feel it, find it, and turn all that versatility into a concrete form.

You don't dream about what comes your way; you dream about something that never came which you bring to yourself.

The road you follow to achieve that dream, the distance travelled, is the *purpose of your life.*

Self-Realization

Don't ever judge your life by failed relationships no matter how much they mattered to you because, at the end of times, you are left with yourself—no one else but yourself.

The one thing you need in that moment is the satisfaction of the life you lived for yourself, making yourself happy the way you wanted to on your own.

You listen to me when I say you are young, your life is about to start, there are many more years left to even start the engine of your life.

Friendship, relationship, and family—all this comes in personal life.

Work comes in professional life.

But what I'm talking about is life, the one that is you.

All I want to say here is, you give chances to people, you give chances to your interests and your hobbies, and you give chances to everything and everybody in this world but, for once, give yourself a chance for yourself, for your life, for your own existence. Trust me, everything will fall into place—things, people, desires, glories, and almost everything.

The day you feel elated and recognize yourself while searching in the mirror, the world will stop turning, it will turn only on your wish.

You will see it happening. Just gather yourself, calm and collected, focused, and just let go of everyone and everything and all shall follow.

You will become the master of your time, and your life will follow you and not vice versa.

You should be so strong and stable in your position that you yourself should be the anchor of your life, and once that happens, all things and every single life crossing your life flows towards you, seeks your support, and eventually makes you realize the magic you can possess by just believing in yourself.

The Very Moment:
The Lost Key

So many times we just sit and think, what will happen tomorrow or the near future? What happened yesterday or further past? And we ignore the present moment and its offerings.

Future—what is future?

It's the present, this moment that is the future of yesterday—all relative.

Past—what is past?

It's again the present, this moment that is the past of tomorrow—again all relative.

If, just for one moment, we stop thinking about yesterday or tomorrow and concentrate and acknowledge the present, the very moment, everything will place itself as we desire.

The key of life is there every passing moment; all you have to do is just pick it up. Stop searching for it because our life is not a maze nor in a straight line. It's just the way we want to see it.

This very moment—this was your future yesterday.

This very moment—this will be your past tomorrow.

So you choose what you want for your future or what you want as your past. It's all in your hands right now. Today, the present, this very moment is everything your life is made of. Don't waste a second of it, and make the best out of it.

The very moment is the lost key of your existence.

The Nucleus: Anger, Nervousness, Modesty, Failure, Chances

Anger

Often people lose their temper to the extent where they regret what they said or did, but words once spoken and actions once executed cannot be taken back, and that leads to the most dangerous of all emotions—regret.

Life with regrets is not the life which has been lived to the best.

If you narrow down all the people you know, you will see that they fall only in two categories—(1) the people you love and care about, the people you want in your life forever, and (2) the people you randomly meet and barely care about or think of.

So regarding the people from the first category, even if you argue with them or be angry with them, you know you will get back together with them sooner or later. One day, one week, or one month, you will be back in touch again.

So what's the point in arguing or fighting with them? You will only be wasting precious time which you could have spent happily, creating wonderful memories.

Regarding the people from the second category, you don't even care about them; it doesn't matter whether they are in your life or not. You don't even think about them, so why waste time even getting angry with them? Don't consume your time thinking how they made you angry and what you should have said or done when, at the end of the day, you don't even care if they are there or not.

If you can differentiate between these two categories, you will never be angry. It won't matter because you would know your priorities and the outcome.

There is an expendable category of in-betweens as well, but they are just there to fill the gaps and be the in-betweens of nothing, the least of our concerns.

A sorted and stable mind is always a step closer to a happier life.

Anger is an emotion which leads to hatred.

Hatred is as strong and as intense an emotion as love.

It's just the darker side of love, and it doesn't take much time to flip the sides.

So think before you get angry because you might be turning off the lights of love towards someone when that someone may be an integral part of your existence.

Nervousness

Nervousness, as we know, is when your heart beats faster, your legs tremble, you're unable to speak correctly. You stammer, perspire, and are just not strong enough to complete what you started, and as a result, everything is left halfway.

The same happens when there is an adrenaline rush. We continue doing what we are doing but with added efforts and enthusiasm, and the result is better than expected.

This happens because we see adrenaline as positive and nervousness as negative.

Change of perception can actually make you realize that adrenaline and nervousness are one and almost the same feeling; it's just that our perceptions differ. I am not talking about the biology of the matter but the feeling of it.

At any stage of life, be it when you are about to finish some work you started or be it doing something you have never done before, our body releases certain hormones; we can't tap into it, but they do generate butterflies in our stomach.

You don't need to fight it; all you have to do is just complete what you started.

Fly with those butterflies. Don't sit back and have any negativity about it. Not many get the chance to fly; consider it an asset.

Name it nervousness or adrenaline, but it surely is an ingredient which is one of the building bricks of our confidence.

You can never be sure of yourself or confident of yourself if you haven't had the feeling that you won't be able to do something but then ended up doing it.

The moment you cross the feeling of nervousness, the task ahead, the reason for your nervousness becomes your forte, and the same result is witnessed when you cross the adrenaline. When the result is the same only after you have conquered your initial feeling, then these two initial feelings have to have something similar as well. The only divide between the two is your perception. Take hold of your perception, and the result will be as desired.

One of the greatest pleasures of life is doing something which you think you cannot.

Modesty

Modesty is not about having assets or materialistic goods or financial mountains and portraying yourself as a very sober and humble individual, helping the underprivileged and presenting it as charity but inside seeing it as a favour with large returns.

Modesty is about being the way you are, whether you have little or a lot, through the way you talk, the way you see, and not by how you act.

Modesty is about having thousands of admires and still believing there are none. And when someone points it out, you get a good feeling, but still you pass it off with a disagreeing smile. It's about having barely any money in your pocket and still willingly giving it to the needy—small quantities but high qualities.

Modesty comes to you when you're most unaware of its existence. Portrayed modesty is in no way modesty; it's a publicity stunt.

In current world conditions, modesty—one of the most humble and genuine distinct emotion of a human—is exploited in the highest degree.

When you are working for your own development by yourself and for yourself, is when you can see yourself in the light of modesty. When you know and have placed every single brick in the building, you will be too busy perfecting it and protecting it. You won't have the time or the space to impose, preach, seek approvals or praises, or proclaim modesty. It's the self-satisfaction that consumes you, and all you reflect to others is pure modesty.

On the day you say it yourself that you are modest, in that very moment, you lost the slightest bit of modesty you had in you.

Failure

It's not about trying to do new projects, trying to achieve your desires, or trying and just not getting it. It's not failure; it's probably that you are doing it the wrong way.

Failure is when you achieve something and lose it.

But even losing something you have is relative if you realize the loopholes and get it back. They're just lessons you learn whether you want to or not.

Mostly, failure is just a state of mind at that moment and is completely revocable.

Winning is a feeling which is necessary in life, and the only way to actually feel and taste of winning is for you to know the taste of failing.

Failure never sets you back; it just pulls you so you can take a leap, a leap to reach the place you have never reached before.

Chances

You say that you've grown old. All the good times have passed you by with the blink of an eye, and now life is not what it used to be; it's so mechanical and so monotonous.

But what you mostly ignore is that you just lose the charm of living with the daily hectic routines.

Nothing has passed you by, but it's actually you who is passing by what makes a good life, which is relative.

Every time you get a chance to be eternally happy, you refuse and say it's not for your age, that you've grown old, and oh, so many reasons. But, tell me now, is it your age of life which is stopping you or your own thinking which is covering all aspects of your personality?

My father always told me that when you receive a call, the power is in your hands to take the call or cancel it, not in the hands of the caller.

So in the same way, before saying or thinking about the famous good old days, which is covered in dust almost every passing day, think again. Are they really gone? Or is it just you who keeps disconnecting the call every time it presents itself?

People say life doesn't give second chances, and if it does, they're very rare. But what are first and second chances? It's all about chances, the chances you take, no first and no second, without expecting a result or returns of it. Take a chance any time and every time you want.

You give life meaning; life doesn't give you meaning.

All the attempts you made for taking a chance in any aspect of your life is the good past which you long for.

Past is what you did right now. Our conversation right now will be a part of your past tomorrow.

Fill your life with the colours you like. Don't wait for life to fill itself on its own because, trust me, life can go on with an empty slate as well.

The Mistuned Harmonics: Artist, Perfection, Freedom

Artist

An *artist* is someone with the perception and empathy and the capability to break just to create and create just to break and make it better.

They evolve every second, creating meanings with their own vision, not understanding them as told.

Creativity in any aspect is the best therapy for all mindsets. It makes you spend time with yourself; it makes you discover the qualities in yourself which you are not even aware of. It teaches you how to depend on someone who will never leave your side, never let you down, and always watch out for you. That someone is *you*.

Every person has an artist in them. Some let it surface, and some just ignore the calling, with the most dangerous fear—the fear of nothing, just a make-believe nothing. Think about it.

Perfection

What is perfection?

It's not being the master of all trades, having the best personality, or having the most luxurious lifestyle.

Nobody is perfect when they meet others' eyes. Everyone wants and expects certain qualities in the other to feel and see them as perfect. But fulfilling a criteria for someone is more like living and behaving according to someone else's perception, and that's not perfection. That's not even close to perfection; that's just compromise with your own self for the good or for the bad. It is an altered way of living.

When you satisfy yourself in your own eyes and you're confident of what you have made yourself, then you are perfect, which is relative to your evolvement and exposure. But it is perfection for the given moment. The further you walk, the more you see and evolve.

Perfection is not stagnant; it keeps on evolving and is very much relative to a given situation or person.

No one was born perfect, nor is anybody going to die perfect.

The constant efforts you take in your entire lifetime just to reach perfection is what makes you perfect in your own way. The awareness of correcting yourself and doing anything from cradle to grave with your best efforts is what makes you reach perfection. It's not only the result that becomes perfect; it's the effort and the conscious fulfilment in your activity that brings perfection.

Perfection in itself is not a quality one can achieve; it is the essence you bring in your life—not by doing what you do, but how you do it. It's just the self-satisfaction which makes you feel perfect about yourself in your personal world.

Once you see it that way, then it's when others see it your way too.

Freedom

Freedom is one of the most relative and misunderstood terms which we perceive as well as try to practise almost all our lives.

Breaking the shackles, breaking the law, crossing all boundaries, and extending oneself beyond their limits do not define freedom.

Neither behaving rebelliously or recklessly nor being an outlaw defines freedom.

Mostly, people misunderstand it. Some may think it's the rules and regulations that take away their freedom, and some say that unless they live alone, they can never achieve true freedom. Many employees and students say that they are not living with complete freedom.

Well, there is no such thing as true or complete or incomplete freedom. Either it's there, or it's not.

Freedom does not come with your surroundings or environment, your upbringing, or any external force.

Freedom comes from within. It's not a title; it's a feeling.

It's not something that you can demand; it's something that you achieve.

It's not something you display; it's something you radiate.

Evolvement of mind brings along this extraordinary feeling which we desire.

Evolvement comes with maturity; it comes not only with experiences but also when you learn from your experiences and the lessons it brings for you. Age plays no role in mental evolvement.

An evolved mind is a free mind, and a free mind never demands its freedom; it defines it.

Grass is always greener on the other side; hence, people try to fit the lifestyles of the other environments into their current environment. Mixing different environments are serious environmental hazards, and due to the friction, they feel they are not free to execute their ideas. But what they forget is that they are trying to merge different currents. If only it were possible to mix different conditions in one frame, they would feel at ease. But it's not possible, and that is why the other side looks greener. If looked at from an aerial view, it's just a big circle with the same green grass everywhere. Aerial view is your mental evolvement.

Different environments bring out different conditions in lifestyles. Neither are environments built overnight, nor can they be changed overnight.

Hence, you have to evolve your mind internally and not let external illusions pollute it because if they do, you end up being a rebel, an outlaw, and an unfit individual for your specific location. Unknowingly, you'll lose your inherited freedom, the freedom you were born with, because of the manipulated and illusive state known as true freedom.

Few Essentials:
Expectations, Hope,
Desire, Trust, Miracles

Expectations

Expectations can be fulfilled once you are at peace with the acceptance.

Opportunity coming seems insignificant but, when leaving, looks big. So accept things as they come, and then expect them to grow further.

At times, expectations can be very dangerous for one's growth as they make you sit back and just wish that the things you want and dream of will be fulfilled on their own, which is not possible. But after the required effort and work is done, expectation is good as then it's a well-laid vision leading to a promising future.

Expectation from yourself is a way of testing your might in any respective aspect, but expecting anything from anyone else is more of an unknown burden you are loading on the other, which cannot necessarily be fulfilled.

Even if someone gives their level best to fulfil your expectation from them, maybe, just maybe, you expected more. In such cases, the effort of that someone is wasted, and your expectation is broken as well.

So it should be limited to yourself, and any external intervention can lead to disappointment.

Sometimes things don't work out in your favour not because you expected more but because someone else's deliverance was less. But when you are only expecting from yourself, with the right and required efforts, everything falls as planned.

Hope

Hope is just a lead-on of expectations, which leaves you high and dry because it's a doubt between two certainties.

On the positive side, doubt gives you the option to go anywhere without the threat of losing anything, so hope is fine as long as it's used correctly. But before hoping for anything, you should make a choice between a yes or a no and should know what you want before making that choice. Most of the time, the choice made is affected by your known or unknown desires.

Hoping with a positive light is not all that you need to fulfil your desires. A very dedicated and focused approach and hard work are needed to make things materialize in any field, be it personal or professional.

Desire

When you play a game, you play to win and not to lose or be expendable.

The force behind the thought of winning is called *desire.*

There are times, when you actually lose everything you have. The road ahead is not even visible because of so many illusions and problems, but you do gather every bit of yourself and move ahead with or without a path or road to a life ahead. That's the desire carrying you to the future, and with desire, everything becomes possible— not miraculously, but you make everything possible.

Desire is the greatest gift, and thank God for blessing you with it.

Never ever lose it because desire is the unknown force pushing you to wherever you are and where you will be.

Trust

Trust is essentially the term used when unaccountable expectations are being imposed unintentionally on one individual, and as pure as it is, it's equally vulnerable to exploitation.

If controlled, the amount of expectation, even in the worst case, can do no harm.

Usually after being betrayed once, you exactly know how much to expect and how much to accept.

Trust is the emotion which exists but cannot be displayed or said. You do things which the other has to recognize, and gradually that mutual efforts and recognition builds into trust.

No matter how hard you try, it will be in vain if the other refuses to acknowledge it.

Trust in itself is a big burden on anyone and everybody— for the one who trusts and for the one who is trusted— because it comes with a lot of expectations and hopes and, most of the time, the expectations can be higher and the deliverance might be lower. In such cases, even after the best efforts, the expectations are not met, and no one does anything wrong, yet the trust is tarnished.

It's not a one-way street, but if it becomes one, then the pure trust becomes a burden for the other. Under any or all circumstances, trust has to be mutual.

Miracles

It's like you have an inbuilt cutter; it resharpens the blunt, and it makes what's already sharp glitter.

It's the magic you have inside yourself but refuse to acknowledge.

You keep praying to God for miracles to happen, but you keep forgetting that you are the *miracle.*

Realizing the miracle in yourself as well takes time, but just before it takes shape, you lose your faith and zeal to continue.

When hard work with focus and dedication and ultimate belief in yourself is put into anything you do, the results are miraculous and are far more than your initial desired results.

Just keep the faith in yourself and see how everything changes for good.

Something about Love

Seeking the companionship of another can have multiple reasons, and in most circumstances, it's for fighting your loneliness. The path people usually choose is marriage. But what is marriage? It's basically an extension of celebrating the love you share with your partner. It's mostly misunderstood, which leads to disastrous results.

Love is a term given to this unknown feeling. Sometimes infatuation is what love becomes, and sometimes it's a label you give to be with someone.

Love in itself is nothing, and then it's everything. But what is love? Love is a journey, and only sincere care for your partner can make this journey possible. Love is nothing without care, but care is everything despite nothing supplementing it. When you truly care for a person, you have no obstacles to overcome; you have no space for friction. It's all smooth, but only if it is shared mutually.

Nine out of ten failed marriages happen because their care for each other was missing.

How can you hurt someone you love? Well, you do hurt your partner more than often, but you never hurt someone you care for. Hence, it is almost impossible for any sadness to surface itself.

A companionship shared for no subtle or apparent reasons always lasts the longest. Loneliness, infatuation, attraction, or misunderstood love has the possibility of fading away once you take away the reason for your movement. Your movement stops. But unconditional care, a genuine care, never ends, and it comes with no conscious or subconscious requirement. It goes on, and it goes on through all the years you spend with your partner in such feelings. You look back, and you call it love. Love you shared, love you gave, love you received, and then this unknown emotion becomes known and again indefinable.

The Other Side of
Your Reality

When you are around random people, the situations are comfortable, and you act upon your wish. You meet them easily, talk, and just hang around together with no troubles or wait.

But when you actually come across the right person, *the one* for you, it isn't that easy. God won't give it to you until he tests you and sees if you have the patience to contain it and the strength to stick by it, thick or thin.

Anything or anyone that comes easily in your life you don't value it as much as you would value something or someone for which or whom you have worked hard and patiently waited for.

Human tendency is such that anything that's served within easy reach is not satisfying but anything that's put at a distance or any difficult situation incites all the desires and passion to work together to achieve it. But most of the time, the test you have to take for the desired results is difficult, and many fail to complete it.

Well, think again. If something does not come easy, maybe you are not equipped to contain it and hold it and secure it. So the journey to reach it, the difficulties faced, and the patience tested make you strong and wise enough to cherish it and protect it for yourself.

Give a child a fragile glass toy, and he will break it. But let him grow over the years, just looking at it but not being allowed to touch it, and he will learn to value it. And when he gets it, he will keep it safe and sound, not allowing even a scratch to be on it.

The point which we normally skip is that anything and everything in this world is possible. All you need to do is gather your focus and find the direction. God only protects the results of your dreams until you achieve them yourself and you are fully equipped with the knowledge to contain it and secure it.

This applies to the people you want in your life and to all the achievements you want to conceive.

Everything is interconnected, but you can only see one link of the chain at the given time. Look back, and you can see the entire chain. But at the same time, look ahead, and it's just that very moment.

This is *the other side of your reality.* What you can see is a fraction of what you can't.

Betrayal to Self

Sometimes you are living your life which is justified to the world but is a *betrayal to self.*

Good job, good home, good car, and few friends—what else does a person need? This is what is usually said about an individual who is leading such a life. But it's not necessarily true that satisfaction for some is satisfaction for others.

It's not always about the security that you live by. There is an invisible spark which keeps on ticking every now and then, and mostly, people ignore it. But some people tap it and make it a motive to realize that spark and bring a revolution to their lives.

Remember, sometimes while trying to raise the curtains from the unknown, you end up excluding yourself from something you want, just to cherish it with its full taste later. Then in the meantime, you learn something—only you would know not the rules of living your life but actually the trick of living it the right way.

Anyone else just won't understand, will straight away judge you, and will reach conclusions which you won't be at peace with because mostly people live by others' perception over their own.

It's all a web of disaster, leading to a highly dissatisfactory life, but still you don't question and rather just settle with what is apparently the right way, the right way designed by a handful of people with their limited vision practised in their own life.

It's easier to betray yourself because you are the only one who will understand and won't question yourself, but sometimes in life, you will face the truth, which will be far stronger than your facts. That will be the time when you will realize that the time you betrayed yourself with make-believe ways was when you ended your free life and started sustaining an empty life with no vision of your own.

Always remember that you are only answerable to yourself and no one else. All your actions, decisions, and choices come back to you at the end of the day. Prepare your answers for all that you do. Stop betraying yourself before your inner self starts betraying you.

The Game: Blame

Whenever a problem occurs, it brings out the divisional markings amongst people. Usually, there are two kinds of people—the ones who solve the problem and the others who find someone to blame it on.

Here we are talking about the condemned and the most self-destructive people who as well are a threat to the system (which consists of many more individuals). Their evasive nature only causes confusion and commotion in the most well-organized structures as well as their own lives, leaving nothing but the problem that occurred in the first place unsolved.

Problematic situations occur at home, workplace, or any possible environment, and such people are present to give their due evasion towards solutions and create a mountain of a mole hill.

One should never evade or look for reasons to escape a situation. A problem can only be solved with a solution; it's as simple as that.

The nature of blaming somebody for your own problem instead of focusing on the solution of it is as grave and as destructive as the legend of the mark of Cain.

Cain, being the firstborn of this world and after his actions of slaying his own brother for reasons such as jealousy, was condemned with a mark which made him a nomad and a lonesome man, being excluded from his family and all human interactions.

So here the mark is on the people who play the blame game every time something wrong occurs, not knowing that eventually they'll be rejected by all and will live a life with no consequence and being a burden on others. So stop this destructive nature before it isolates you from all your surroundings.

If you want a life which is respectable and dependable, then start with the simple step of taking responsibility for your actions, and if any given situation goes wrong, never ever find someone to blame it on. Not only will you be able to live your life with dignity, but you would also become an asset for everyone else's life as well.

It all starts with little things and situations. Sometimes the ones who love you take the blame for you, and sometimes your role is just ignored without reason. But these little incidences take shape in your mind and become your defence mechanism, which further down is seen as a personality trait.

Even the best of relationships take a sour turn because of such behaviour. The behaviour conflicts your inner self with your outer self, leaving spaces—dark empty spaces. And these spaces, we usually call these demons inside your mind.

So don't take advantage of someone's concern as, in the long run, you will be poisoning your own life.

Live

Live because you are going to die someday.

Life is incomplete if you don't live it; floating and just existing is not what living means.

All the vivid or faded memories you have are the only times when you actually lived your life, and it's so beautiful that they become memories which still makes you smile whenever you think about them.

For every passing moment in every passing day, you make a conscious choice or a subconscious choice, whether or not you are going to be happy. Do what you love, and do what you really want to do.

Most of the time, your choice is a big no for everything, and that choice comes from the subconscious because of the everyday mundane activities and because of the current monotonous wave in the world, distracting the other to rule the other.

Everything will go on with or without you.

But you will stop without yourself, without you.

So you should be the single most important concern for yourself.

When you change, only then will the world around you change. It's a chain reaction, the domino effect.

Do what makes you happy, and your happiness will make you do and say things which will make others happy.

Hence comes the long-awaited change, the change of heart.

The power that makes you choose love over hate, happiness over sadness, light over dark, life over death.

If you lived your life—that is, lived it happily—then death is just a bonus to make you eternal, eternal with the mindset of a happily lived life.

Be a part of this revolution; it's not over yet.

The Fine Line:
Vanity and Waste

There is nothing wrong in being happy, in acknowledging the facts, such as being pleasant and blessed with an attractive appearance, having innate or acquired qualities, and achieving success through hard work.

When others praise you, it's a compliment, and when you acknowledge it yourself, its vanity, a sin.

But if you won't recognize your own self, in all probabilities, it'll go ignored by everyone, but when you do appreciate yourself, only then will others do as well.

How you treat yourself is how others treat you.

However, anything done in extremes is dangerous. Overindulgence in the qualities of oneself will saturate the evolvement of the mind, and the already possessed qualities will gradually decay into nothing because there is a very fine line between vanity and waste and you have to manage to be in between these two fallouts. We cannot condemn pride in oneself as it'll waste your potential because of lack of appreciation for oneself, and you cannot even overindulge in it as again it'll lead to vanity; the road ahead is waste.

The balance should be maintained between being vain and being ignorant. Vanity will make you cross the line and lead you to waste, and ignorance will make you underestimate yourself and will not let you realize your own qualities and gradually will guide you to waste into nothing.

Cherish what you are blessed with, acknowledge it, and protect it.

You are not rich because someone else is poor.

You are not tall just because someone is short.

You are not happy just because someone is sad.

You are whatever you are because of yourself, your own choice, and not because of someone else.

Your position is defined by you and not by some comparison with someone else.

What Would You Say?

W ell, the fairer share of the world believes you to be successful when you drive a fancy car, own a beautiful house, have a big bank account, dine at the fanciest of places, and the list goes on.

Such examples definitely define your survival instinct and your place in this highly paced and competitive world. But for all those, including me, who do believe in the superpower, the ultimate source, God and all our perspectives reaching the same conclusion. What would you say to the mighty when face-to-face with him? What did you do in this life you lived? What was your purpose, spending money that you made yourself?

Nothing is wrong in an honest living, but living honestly without any purpose is like floating in this infinite space for no real good reason. When you're with the Almighty, will you even be able to look at him eye to eye? Do you know what you will say when asked, 'What did you do all your life?'

In all honesty, worldly materials don't take you anywhere after you die. You cannot impress God with your fancy cars, nor can you take him for fine dining. The only thing that will even be close to your merit will be the way you lived your life. Was it honest? Was it lived with dignity and loyalty? Or was it consumed by greed, dissatisfaction, betrayal, and double standards?

The priorities in our lives are adulterated, and in order to heal them, you have to understand them.

Priorities can be understood with the help of this four-step story.

Every human has four friends in life. The first friend leaves you the moment you die. The second friend is with you till your final resting place. The third friend prays for you and remembers you till the end of their lives. But the fourth friend goes where you go—heaven or hell or the oblivion—your only companion for eternity.

Who are these friends?

The first friend is money; the second friend, your acquaintances or the companions you choose; the third friend, your family; and the fourth friend, your karma.

So prioritize these four friends wisely. Only one of them will leads you and be with you forever.

You have a choice—while you are still alive—to change it, to make your life worthwhile.

It's You in the Mirror

The truth was a mirror in the hands
of God. It fell, and broke into pieces.
Everybody took a piece of it, and they
looked at it and thought they had the
truth.

Jalal ad-Din Muhammad Rumi

Mostly, this statement can be understood in
multiple ways. It's like everybody has a piece of truth
with them, or everybody is right in their own way. And if
all the pieces are put back together, we can find peace in
that complete truth. Well, the only constant I see here is
that truth is not relative but relativity is the truth. How I
see it is that a mirror is a mirror. Even if you break it into

a million of pieces and you join them back all together, the end result will be the same; it remains a mirror, and a mirror just shows your own reflection.

So ultimately, the truth is *you*. Once you accept this truth about yourself, you can find peace within yourself, and once you are peaceful inside, that's when you can bring peace outside.

Patience

Patience is the leap of faith between the tangible and the intangible. It's an innate or an acquired quality, and irrespective of its source, one must possess it.

It's a place where nothing happens, and nothing is a place where everything happens. It's the reference point of your inner self meeting your outer self. It's a place where you retrospect and you reflect. It's the centre of you, and the centre of you is the centre of everything that you do and have in your life.

Patience is not practised. Patience is required while practising. Patience makes you practise.

It's not a virtue you achieve. Patience helps build your virtues. It's stillness that makes you move. It's the back story of all your doings in your entire existence.

It's the one quality that's not measured in time; it can only be understood or measured after the wait is over.

Sometimes in life, you are in situations or amongst some people where the stride is not in your favour. Reacting itself is understood as overreacting. There at that very moment, the ability that releases you from that situation or people is *patience*. Silence as well carries a message, and patience is the key to that code.

To be the master of anything, be it professional or personal, you need to have complete understanding of it, and to understand something or someone, you have to go through the process of reaching its core and coming back without even remotely altering the subject. The essence of this procedure, the ability that helps you achieve it successfully is *patience.*

Patience is not something that slows you down or holds you back. It's the force that makes you invincible and unstoppable.

Have patience.

Silence

What language do the wind, water, or fire use? Every human feels them regardless of their origins. They make you feel them.

Every bit of nature communicates through *silence.*

When you love someone, the words are not enough to make the other feel the love. To make someone feel, you have to say it with silence.

Acknowledge the other side of your visual world; you will realize that being with someone in person is a mere formality, just a visual satisfaction, whereas the real communication happens when the energies of the individuals meet.

Energies are felt, not seen or heard. They have no shape or size, no requirements or expectations. They are simple and straight. They either merge, or they deflect.

The languages we created are boundaries to our imaginations; they are the restrictions between one human to the other.

Your soul knows how to communicate silently.

The most pleasurable moments come to you silently.

Your feelings make you who you are as an individual, and your feelings communicate in silence.

Accepting silence is the essence you add to your life, which makes you experience every second of the day and gives meaning to the gaps you feel in your existence.

In order to feel, you have to start understanding silence.

Silence is divine. Silence is the divine language, the language your soul speaks, and your soul is the reflection of God in you.

Most of the unexplainable emotions in life are the emotions which no words can justify; only silence makes the other feel it too.

God communicates to us in silence. He understands every language we humans have created, and still we fail to understand the one universal language he created.

Anything unseen is not believed, but many untold emotions, even if not heard, are felt.

Silence is the most important language we all must know and practise.

It will give meaning to your life.

The End—That's When It All Begins

'When everything stops, time moves, and time changes everything. That means nothing stops, but it feels we're stuck at a standstill.'

So is it that all functions at some point in life actually come to a halt and time doesn't exist, or is it the other way around?

This is the feeling mostly everybody faces after they encounter one of this life's most challenging yet inevitable part—death, death of someone very near and dear.

'Only if we got another chance to spend more time together . . .' So much was unsaid. So much was left undone. We're always waiting for that perfect moment to say something or do something, but then comes this undefined phenomenon of life which, in more precise words, is the end of the life in our physical form, the most feared yet guaranteed fact of life—death.

You see it almost every day. Someone or the other is dying, but still it's something you can never get used to. It's new to each as it happens with their loved ones. The anxiety and the lost vision which comes along with it is only understood once suffered.

After losing my father, I realized and suffered certain uncertainties of life, and after learning and forcefully facing them, I had to keep them inside as when these lessons are taught, they make you value the moments and the better way of living but not with another chance. You're left with just a message to pass to the others who are still blessed with their families and are unaware of it's brutal and heart-wrenching end.

You are so lost in the monotony of life that you forget about your priorities.

You're in search for a perfect life, happiness, and satisfaction by leaving it all behind, just to realize that what you left behind was what you were looking for. But this realization happens only after your life is ready to give you the lesson which you can only pass on but cannot practise yourself.

Time is a great healer. Really? Is it?

The void is always there, but by trying not to see it and feel it because it's too painful and because sometimes you have become too numb to feel, you distract yourself with various activities. So it's the distraction that momentarily heals your hurt, but the scars are there, which you always keep because some scars are worth dying for.

Time as we know is nothing yet everything.

If you take out the batteries from your clock, your clock will stop, but time won't.

In the same way, if you choose not to live, you won't live, but your life will go on with or without your consent.

So before trying to wallow in sorrow, look at the brighter side of it. Maybe you were not fortunate enough to learn it earlier, but it's never too late to share your sorrows with the people who are not exposed to this feeling as yet because your sorrows, which may seem devastating to you, might actually be an eye-opener for some, and that might change their life forever.

Great lessons come to you when you are most unaware of them and most unprepared to accept and adapt them. Don't keep this learning deep inside; it will gradually decay you. Share them and give your life meaning by living it for yourself, and then many will live because of the inspiration you will be generating around you.

Dreams

The page for *dreams*, I leave empty as only *you* will decide what you will dream of. It's as simple as this blank page. It's all an empty slate; colour it with your soul. Dream. Dream until you achieve it, and when you do, dream more.

Just for You

Sometimes you have to open your eyes to see it, and sometimes you have to close your eyes to feel it.

The difference between the two is just a blink, but if the difference is recognized, it becomes a life-changing force. It brings out the harmony which is always missing in one's life, the harmony to empathize with any given situation or person. Empathy is an essence which is required to enter your existence without any friction.

All it takes is *just a moment*, just a moment that makes you forget all your problems, all your hardships, all that was unbearable. That one moment makes you forget everything—*everything*. If you face it, then seize it and live it. In that very moment, your whole life can be defined!

Life is all about perceptions, and once you acknowledge that, you can have the power to change your perceptions. While doing that, you're changing your life. It'll attract and bring *chances* and *choices* in your life, and that will lead you to your alpha self, the best version of yourself.

Being ambitious, driven by achieving success in everything you do, is not wrong. It's the best purpose one can have. But while you're on the path of achieving it, never forget who you are. Your ambitions belong to you; you don't belong to your ambitions.

The toughest decisions we make in our lives either by choice or by external pressure turns out to be the corrections to lead us to our actual paths. So whether it's caused by you or caused by someone else, *you* must make those decisions. Once you do, you will see that they actually are just deflections to bring our own deflections in order, hence leading you to the actually destination you have to reach, be it personal or professional.

Building a wall around you just to protect yourself from getting hurt is a natural defence of an individual. There will be many people who care for you or love you and want to be with you, but the wall built restricts them.

But trust me on this, it may not be today, but whenever it happens, you will just smile to yourself. It doesn't matter how tall or strong the wall you build around yourself is. Believe me, thousands will walk back or just give up, but someday, someone will come, and for whom your wall will come crashing down on its own. If it won't, then he or she will break it down brick by brick and reach out for the real you with or without your consent, heal all the wounds inside, and fill all the missing pieces.

All you need to do is be true to yourself and live each day without regrets. In the meantime, magic will happen, and you would be in the perfect circle with the one your soul seeks.

The only way to understand about yourself is to push the potential inside you and put it to use, and once you can say that, I did it all on my own—all on my own. Then for you, even a cheap ticket or an expensive house measures the same. I bought it. I did it on my own. It all becomes the same; only the cost differs. Money is extremely important only till you don't have it. But once you have it, you don't value what you have, and then the search begins for the things money cannot buy.

Money and materials are to be used, and people are to be cared for, but it's the other way around in the world today. However, only if you remember how it was when you had none, you will own it after getting it; it doesn't own you.

Everyone is better than some, and some are better than everyone. It's a circle, and you can never escape it. But if you step above it, you're no longer in the circle, and the only way to step above it is by how much you have in life that you can't sell or use.

All that your mind can perceive, you can achieve, and there is nothing in this world that can stop you. Only your own misconceptions are your hurdles.

Either you know, or you don't. Don't care about what others think. Only care about what you think. What you know, no one can deny, and what you don't know, learn. The only issue here is, learn from where? Because once you learn something, you can't unlearn it. So instead of going with what others saw and delivered with the limitations of their imagination and perception, create your very own because only you know what you want and how you want it. Meanings are like boats. Till the time they float, they float, and then they sink. But if you created it, you can create it again. But if you were influenced, you will look for another source, and sources can be manipulated. Believe only in yourself.

Whenever you are about to say or do something, you know if it's right or wrong. Let that feeling emerge from within and merge right back in you. It'll direct you about what to say and do.

You are a wonderful person, and you have a bright future right at your feet because you know what you want and how to get it.

You are complete as one, and you are incomplete with some.

So it's time to love the person, you made yourself and do something for that person, for his or her happiness, welfare, and peace.

Sometimes in life, even after knowing the situations inside out, you want a second opinion not because it will change anything but for the reassurance of faith in yourself and divine intervention.

One life is about you and is mostly about all the situations you face in your life. Whenever in doubt, you can silently ask your question, and just open this book and read the part which meets your first glance. You might find the direction you've been ignoring or maybe are unaware of.

Believe before you question, and ask with your sincere heart. I am sure God will find his own medium to reach *you*.

Printed in the United States
By Bookmasters